Family
Documents

C0-CCH-028

What they are
Where they are

This is a record of the personal documents of

Name _____

Name _____

Street _____ *Apt*_____

*City*_____

State/Prov _____ *Zip/Post Code*_____

*Tel (___)*_____ *Fax (___)*_____

E-Mail _____

Date of last entry   1 _____

2 _____   3 _____

Family Documents

What they are
Where they are

Walter and Esther Dueck

Foreword	Ross T. Taylor
Cover	Emma Duncan
Poetry	Drew Gordon

Waterside House Publishing
714 Vine Street
St. Catharines ON Canada L2M 6Z6
(905) 935-5047

Canadian Cataloguing in Publication Data

Dueck, Walter, date
    Family documents: what they are, where they are

ISBN 0-9682628-0-5 (Paper)
ISBN 0 9682628-1-3 (Hardcover)

          1. Records—Management. 2. Diaries (Blank-books).
I. Dueck, Esther, date II. Title.

TX147.D83 1997   640   C97-900873-5

Copyright © 1997 by Walter & Esther Dueck

All rights reserved. No part of this publication may be reproduced, stored in a retrieval system or transmitted, in any form or by any means, electronic, mechanical, photocopying, recording, or otherwise, without the prior permission of the publisher.

Third Printing

Printed on acid-free paper

Acknowledgements

We are indebted to family members, friends and professionals
whose help and advice we value.

FOREWORD

Perhaps the most subtle change most of us will face during our lifetime is the inevitable realization that we cannot remember everything anymore. For years we have operated on the basis that we know where everything is, deal with it appropriately and can put our finger on every important document, identification number or bank account whenever we need it.

By the time we become aware it is getting tougher to remember it all, we are probably already spending significant amounts of our time looking for things and increasing our stress level. If we redirected some of that time into creative stress reduction by recording it all in a book, we could enjoy a lot more of the rest of our lives.

Considering the amount of time and frustration this could save you and me, imagine the relief this would create for our heirs and family members who may become responsible to look after us and/or our affairs in later years. They might not have the benefit of our memory, albeit deteriorating or inconsistent. Without an accurate record, they could be operating pretty much in the dark.

Where people have made no effort to record the most important information of their lives, their children or heirs often spend enormous amounts of time trying to piece it all together. Tragically, large sums of money go unclaimed every year because there is just not enough information available to locate it. This is so unnecessary!

Walter and Esther have made this task much easier by producing this incredible book to assist you in giving your family the gift of comfort and peace of mind. This way everything you have worked so hard to obtain stays in your family. Your financial assets will not be lost or end up in dormant accounts. Insurance and benefits for which you have paid premiums will be easy to claim. Everything you or your heirs are entitled to can be preserved if all the necessary information is readily accessible.

With this book, your life and the lives of your closest family members just got better!

Ross T. Taylor, CFP, CLU. CH.F.C.
Certified Financial Planner
Chartered Financial Consultant

PREFACE

This book grew out of our own need to have a complete list of our 'family documents' and some clear directions about their location. Before we went to Europe for a one-year educational assignment we wrote a draft copy of this book, filled it out and left it with the children. At the time we had no success locating a published product that would do the job for us. Subsequently we were encouraged to formalize our working model into this expanded format. Our discussions with professionals in the financial and legal fields convinced us that this book was long overdue.

Family Documents has been designed for specific purposes: to be the main information centre for a person's family documents and to provide essential information for future reference. It's format is easy to understand and use.

We believe that the data recorded here will be important not only to the person who completes it, but also to the family and executors who read it and need it.

It is a way to remember.

TABLE OF CONTENTS ℂℨ

HOW TO USE THIS BOOK ⟡

◆ This is a practical book to use for collecting and listing important personal and financial information about yourself.

◆ It can help you record and organize documents and information about your home and your safe deposit box .

◆ How *much* information you put into this book *is your choice.*

◆ Use pencil where you may wish to change or update information.

◆ Always keep this book in a safe place. Tell someone in your family where you keep this book.

◆ Some people may wish to give a second completed book to a family member in case of an emergency.

◆ This book or a second completed book will be useful to your executor.

◆ In some cases, e.g. blended families, each spouse may wish to complete a book.

◆ This book is not meant to be used as a will.

◆ This book is an ideal gift for young people, boomers and their parents. It is not about *how much* one has but rather about *where* a person's documents and property are located.

INFORMATION ABOUT US ⍵

My Legal Name

Given name	Middle	Surname

Name change/Nick names _____

Birth Date & Place _____

Location of Birth Cert. _____

          Marriage Cert. _____

Can. S.I.N. _____

Prov.Health No. _____

Can. Passport No. _____

U.S. Soc. Security No. _____

U.S. Health Care Provider ID No. _____

U.S. Medicare Insur. No. _____

U.S. Passport No. _____

Driver's License No. _____

Names of my

Father _____

Mother _____ Nee _____

Other _____

My Spouse's Legal Name

Given name   Middle   Surname

Name change/Nick names _____

Birth Date & Place _____

Location of Birth Cert. _____

Marriage Cert. _____

Can. S.I.N. _____

Prov.Health No. _____

Can. Passport No. _____

U.S. Soc. Security No. _____

U.S. Health Care Provider ID No. _____

U.S. Medicare Insur. No. _____

U.S. Passport No. _____

Driver's License No. _____

Names of my

Father _____

Mother _____ Nee _____

Other _____

CHILDREN ℃

Legal Name _____
  Birth
  Date & Place _____
                                   Postal/Zip
  Address _____ Code _____

  Tel. (___) _____ Fax (___) _____

  S.I.N./ Soc.Sec.No. _____

  Other _____

Legal Name _____
  Birth
  Date & Place _____
                                   Postal/Zip
  Address _____ Code _____

  Tel. (___) _____ Fax (___) _____

  S.I.N./ Soc.Sec.No. _____

  Other _____

Legal Name _____
  Birth
  Date & Place _____
                                   Postal/Zip
  Address _____ Code _____

  Tel. (___) _____ Fax (___) _____

  S.I.N./ Soc.Sec.No. _____

  Other _____

Legal Name
Birth
Date & Place

Address   Postal/Zip
                                                     Code

Tel. (___)   Fax (___)

S.I.N./ Soc.Sec.No.

Other

Legal Name
Birth
Date & Place

Address   Postal/Zip
                                                     Code

Tel. (___)   Fax (___)

S.I.N./ Soc.Sec.No.

Other

Legal Name
Birth
Date & Place

Address   Postal/Zip
                                                     Code

Tel. (___)   Fax (___)

S.I.N./ Soc.Sec.No.

Other

Additional information about Children on next page.

NOTES

NOTES

CONTACTS ❀

Executor _____

Address _____

    Tel. (___) _____ Fax (___) _____

    Has a copy of the will.   Yes ☐   No ☐

Executor _____

    Address _____

    Tel. (___) _____ Fax (___) _____

    Has a copy of the will.   Yes ☐   No ☐

Lawyer _____

    Address _____

    Tel. (___) _____ Fax (___) _____

    Has a copy of the will.   Yes ☐   No ☐

Financial Consultant _____

    Address _____

    Tel. (___) _____ Fax (___) _____

NOTES _____

Accountant _____

Address _____

Tel. (___) _____ Fax (___) _____

Accountant _____

Address _____

Tel. (___) _____ Fax (___) _____

Power of Attorney

Name _____

Tel. (___) _____ Fax (___) _____

Name _____

Tel. (___) _____ Fax (___) _____

Name _____

Tel. (___) _____ Fax (___) _____

NOTES _____

_____

_____

_____

_____

Additional *information on next page.*

NOTES

DOCUMENTS ⟡

SAFE DEPOSIT BOX

Location _____

    Box No. _____ Key location _____

Location _____

    Box No. _____ Key location _____

Location _____

    Box No. _____ Key location _____

Contents of safe deposit box/es are listed at the end of this book.

Yes ☐   No ☐   (See page 50) Other location is _____

Duplicate copies of important papers are held at

    Home   Yes ☐   No ☐

    Location _____

    Other places _____

NOTES on other documents _____

_____

_____

FUNERAL ARRANGEMENTS

Details are outlined in the will   Yes ☐   No ☐

Plans completed with _____

Tel. (___)_____   Fax (___)_____

Other arrangements _____

_____

_____

_____

CEMETERY PLOT/S

Own   Yes ☐   No ☐

Location _____

Contact _____

Tel. (___)_____   Fax (___)_____

NOTES on other documents _____

_____

_____

_____

_____

PROPERTY WE OWN ❃

Home Address
(Principal Residence)

Deed located at

Insurance Co. _____ Tel. (___) _____

Policy located at

Other Property such as ◆ art, antiques, boats, cars, coins, cottage, commercial, jewelry, land.

◆ _____ Location _____

Deed located at

Insurance Co. _____ Tel. (___) _____

Policy located at

◆ _____ Location _____

Deed located at

Insurance Co. _____ Tel. (___) _____

Policy located at

◆ _____ Location _____

_____

Deed located at _____

Insurance Co._____ Tel. (___) _____

Policy located at _____

◆ _____ Location _____

_____

Deed located at _____

Insurance Co._____ Tel. (___) _____

Policy located at _____

◆ _____ Location _____

_____

Deed located at _____

Insurance Co._____ Tel. (___) _____

Policy located at _____

NOTES _____

_____

_____

PROPERTY

◆ _____ Location _____

_____

Deed located at _____

Insurance Co._____ Tel. (___) _____

Policy located at _____

◆ _____ Location _____

_____

Deed located at _____

Insurance Co._____ Tel. (___) _____

Policy located at _____

◆ _____ Location _____

_____

Deed located at _____

Insurance Co._____ Tel. (___) _____

Policy located at _____

NOTES _____

_____

_____

Inter-family loans and/or private investments

LIFE INSURANCE ∽

Policy holder _____

    Life insured _____

    Company _____ Policy No. _____

    Beneficiary _____ Amount _____

Policy holder _____

    Life insured _____

    Company _____ Policy No. _____

    Beneficiary _____ Amount _____

Policy holder _____

    Life insured _____

    Company _____ Policy No. _____

    Beneficiary _____ Amount _____

Policy holder _____

    Life insured _____

    Company _____ Policy No. _____

    Beneficiary _____ Amount _____

NOTES _____

Policy holder _____

Life insured _____

Company _____ Policy No. _____

Beneficiary _____ Amount _____

Policy holder _____

Life insured _____

Company _____ Policy No. _____

Beneficiary _____ Amount _____

Policy holder _____

Life insured _____

Company _____ Policy No. _____

Beneficiary _____ Amount _____

Policy holder _____

Life insured _____

Company _____ Policy No. _____

Beneficiary _____ Amount _____

NOTES _____

OTHER INSURANCE ❧

- ◆ Health, Auto, Apartment, Travel, Credit Cards, Burial, Mortgage, Warranties and others

◆ _____ Company _____

Address _____

Tel. (____) _____ Policy No. _____

◆ _____ Company _____

Address_____

Tel. (____) _____ Policy No. _____

◆ _____ Company _____

Address_____

Tel. (____) _____ Policy No. _____

◆ _____ Company _____

Address_____

Tel. (____) _____ Policy No. _____

◆ _____ Company _____

Address_____

Tel. (____) _____ Policy No. _____

NOTES _____

OTHER INSURANCE

◆ _____ Company _____

Address _____

Tel. (___) _____ Policy No. _____

◆ _____ Company _____

Address _____

Tel. (___) _____ Policy No. _____

◆ _____ Company _____

Address _____

Tel. (___) _____ Policy No. _____

◆ _____ Company _____

Address _____

Tel. (___) _____ Policy No. _____

NOTES _____

_____

_____

_____

_____

_____

INCOME SOURCES ❧

Employer _____

    Address _____

Employer _____

    Address _____

Pension Plans

1 _____

2 _____

U.S. Soc. Sec. *   Yes ☐   No ☐

Can. Pen. Plan *   Yes ☐   No ☐

Other _____

Old Age Security * _____

* For USA Social Security : Contact nearest US Soc. Sec. Dept. office.
Canada Pension Plan / Old Age Security : Contact nearest office of
Human Resources Development Canada

Rental

Property _____

    Location _____

Property _____

    Location _____

Annuities

Issuing
Company _____

Policy No._____ Beneficiary _____

Issuing
Company _____

Policy No._____ Beneficiary _____

Issuing
Company _____

Policy No._____ Beneficiary _____

NOTES / *Additional income sources information*

_____

_____

_____

_____

_____

_____

_____

INCOME SOURCES - SPOUSE ☙

Employer _____

    Address _____

Employer _____

    Address _____

Pension Plans

    1 _____

    2 _____

    U.S. Soc. Sec. *   Yes ☐   No ☐

    Can. Pen. Plan *   Yes ☐   No ☐

    Other _____

Old Age Security * _____

* For USA Social Security : Contact nearest US Soc. Sec. Dept. office.
Canada Pension Plan / Old Age Security : Contact nearest office of
Human Resources Development Canada

Rental

    Property _____

    Location _____

    Property _____

    Location _____

Annuities

Issuing
Company _____

Policy No. _____ Beneficiary _____

Issuing
Company _____

Policy No. _____ Beneficiary _____

Issuing
Company _____

Policy No. _____ Beneficiary _____

NOTES | ***Additional*** *income sources information*

_____

_____

_____

_____

_____

_____

_____

TAX-SHELTERED INVESTMENTS ❧

Types may include GICs/CDs, Mutual Funds, Segregated Funds
and others

Investment Firm _____

    Address _____ Tel. (____) _____

    Location of Documents _____

    Account No. _____ Type _____

Investment Firm _____

    Address _____ Tel. (____) _____

    Location of Documents _____

    Account No. _____ Type _____

Investment Firm _____

    Address _____ Tel. (____) _____

    Location of Documents _____

    Account No. _____ Type _____

Investment Firm _____

    Address _____ Tel. (____) _____

    Location of Documents _____

    Account No. _____ Type _____

TAX-SHELTERED INVESTMENTS

Investment Firm _____

    Address _____ Tel. (___)_____

    Location of Documents _____

    Account No. _____ Type _____

Investment Firm _____

    Address _____ Tel. (___)_____

    Location of Documents _____

    Account No. _____ Type _____

Investment Firm _____

    Address _____ Tel. (___)_____

    Location of Documents _____

    Account No. _____ Type _____

NOTES _____

_____

_____

_____

_____

_____

OTHER INVESTMENTS / SAVINGS ☞

Types may include GICs/CDs, Stocks/Bonds, Mutual Funds,
Loans/Mortgages and others

Investment Firm _____

Address _____ Tel. (___) _____

Location of Documents _____

Account No. _____ Type _____

Investment Firm _____

Address _____ Tel. (___) _____

Location of Documents _____

Account No. _____ Type _____

Investment Firm _____

Address _____ Tel. (___) _____

Location of Documents _____

Account No. _____ Type _____

Investment Firm _____

Address _____ Tel. (___) _____

Location of Documents _____

Account No. _____ Type _____

Investment Firm _____

Address _____ Tel. (____) _____

Location of Documents _____

Account No. _____ Type _____

Investment Firm _____

Address _____ Tel. (____) _____

Location of Documents _____

Account No. _____ Type _____

Investment Firm _____

Address _____ Tel. (____) _____

Location of Documents _____

Account No. _____ Type _____

NOTES _____

_____

_____

_____

_____

_____

BANKING INSTITUTIONS ♋

Types of Accounts   Savings, Chequing/Checking,
Business, Foreign Currency and others

NOTE: *Be sure to include all Joint Account names*

NAME of Institution _____

Address _____ Tel. (____) _____

Type of Acct.	Acct. No.	Joint with

NAME of Institution _____

Address _____ Tel. (____) _____

Type of Acct.	Acct. No.	Joint with

NOTES _____

BANKING INSTITUTIONS

NAME of Institution _____

Address _____ Tel. (___)_____

Type of Acct.	Acct. No.	Joint with

NAME of Institution _____

Address _____ Tel. (___)_____

Type of Acct.	Acct. No.	Joint with

NAME of Institution _____

Address _____ Tel. (___)_____

Type of Acct.	Acct. No.	Joint with

DEBTS ℭℬ

MORTGAGES   Yes ☐   No ☐

Documents located at _____

Held by _____ Tel. (____) _____

Address _____

Payment details _____

Held by _____ Tel. (____) _____

Address _____

Payment details _____

Held by _____ Tel. (____) _____

Address _____

Payment details _____

Held by _____ Tel. (____) _____

Address _____

Payment details _____

NOTES _____

_____

_____

LOANS   Yes ☐   No ☐

Documents located at _____

Held by _____ Tel. (___)_____

Address _____

Payment details _____

Held by _____ Tel. (___)_____

Address _____

Payment details _____

Held by _____ Tel. (___)_____

Address _____

Payment details _____

Held by _____ Tel. (___)_____

Address _____

Payment details _____

NOTES _____

_____

_____

_____

CREDIT CARD/CHARGE ACCOUNTS ⌀

Company _____
   Name
   on Card _____ No. _____

Company _____
   Name
   on Card _____ No. _____

Company _____
   Name
   on Card _____ No. _____

Company _____
   Name
   on Card _____ No. _____

Company _____
   Name
   on Card _____ No. _____

Company _____
   Name
   on Card _____ No. _____

Contact *credit card issuer for the possibility of warranty extensions, life and/or accidental death insurance or other benefits that may apply to owners and their family.*

NOTES _____

_____

_____

∽ HOUSEHOLD ACCOUNTS

(List source and phone number)

Electricity _____

Gas / Oil _____

Security System _____

Tel: Line 1 _____

Line 2 _____

Property taxes _____

Water _____

Lawn care _____

TV Cable/Sat. _____

Internet server _____

Other • _____

• _____

Caution. Some regular bills are paid by automatic cheques which will incur significant NSF charges if income or deposits cease and the custodian of the account is not aware of them.

NOTES _____

_____

_____

CHURCHES, CLUBS, SOCIETIES, LODGES, ALUMNI & PROFESSIONAL ORGANIZATIONS ❧

Name

Address

Tel. (＿＿)＿＿＿＿＿＿ Fax (＿＿)＿＿＿＿＿＿

Name

Address

Tel. (＿＿)＿＿＿＿＿＿ Fax (＿＿)＿＿＿＿＿＿

Name

Address

Tel. (＿＿)＿＿＿＿＿＿ Fax (＿＿)＿＿＿＿＿＿

Name

Address

Tel. (＿＿)＿＿＿＿＿＿ Fax (＿＿)＿＿＿＿＿＿

Name

Address

Tel. (＿＿)＿＿＿＿＿＿ Fax (＿＿)＿＿＿＿＿＿

Other

Additional *information on next page.*

CONTENTS OF SAFE DEPOSIT BOX ℭ

List all original documents and other contents. Revise the list when these change. Number the boxes if there are more than one. Keep copies of all important documents in another safe place along with this book.

CONTENTS OF SAFE DEPOSIT BOX

CONTENTS OF SAFE DEPOSIT BOX

MY STORY ☙

Here is a place to briefly record memorable experiences and events in your life.

MY STORY

MY STORY

For those wishing to keep this book in a Safe Deposit Box, complete this form and cut it out.

KEEP THIS HALF IN A SAFE PLACE.

Name_____

My/Our complete personal and financial records are located in

Safe Deposit Box No._____

Bank _____

Address/Location_____

Key No._____ is located _____

_____

✂———————————————————————————————

GIVE THIS HALF TO A FAMILY MEMBER OR EXECUTOR

Name_____

My/Our complete personal and financial records are located in

Safe Deposit Box No._____

Bank _____

Address/Location_____

Key No._____ is located _____

Peace of Mind

There once was a time when our lives were so simple
That dollars were dollars and nickels were nickels
The cookie jar, mattress and old tattered sock
Were more than enough to hide the whole lot.
But how times have changed and how too have we
Now the name of the game is diversity:
Mutual funds, stocks, bonds and GICs
IRAs, RRIFs and RRSPs
Properties, policies and tucked away deeds
Could all make their way to the family tree.
Mortgage and travel and health insurance
To add to your life just a little assurance.
The savings and chequing and off-shore accounts
Do rather well for those other amounts.
Channeling and funneling and pedaling about
Never has cash had as good a workout.
So don't get derailed on a long paper trail
Where few will succeed and many will fail.
Just fill in the blanks of this little book,
You'll reminisce later on the short time it took.
For each finished page brings a smile to your face,
Breathe a sigh of relief, now it's all in one place!

Drew Gordon

What people are saying about **Family Documents**

Chronicling information in this way means financial assets won't be lost or end up in dormant accounts.　　*The Tribune,* Welland

It's like Scotch Tape;　clear, easy to use and everyone needs it.
Jim Buchanan, WICC Radio, Bridgeport, CN

"The will's a start, but there's more to do if you want to ensure your estate is disbursed as you had planned."
Halifax *Chronicle Herald*

When people have completed their will I tell them they've done half the job. Completing *Family Documents* is the other half.
P. Janzen, LLB, Attorney

Family Documents could be worth a million dollars to a family.
J. F. Shearson, Retired International Banker

This book is exactly what I've been looking for.
K. W., Retired librarian

This book will prevent serious and needless aggravation for your spouse and family.　　*The Christian Courier*

Family Documents makes it easy to take pen in hand and list one's possessions under various headings.　　*Seniors Review*

This book is an excellent stewardship tool. It enables you to organize your estate and save your loved ones a great deal of time and confusion in carrying out your wishes.
David Mainse, Crossroads Family of Ministries